I CAN READ ABOUT THE

OCTOPUS

Written by Ellen Schultz

Illustrated by Gloria McKeown

Troll Associates

Have you ever seen an octopus?
Do you know what one looks like?

Some people think that an octopus has
hundreds of giant arms, and many
pairs of eyes.

Others believe that the octopus just lies in wait
on the ocean floor to gobble up divers and boats.

But the truth is
an octopus is really very shy.
If you don't bother it,
it won't bother you.

Many people are frightened by their
strange appearance. But once you
get to understand them, they are
really quite interesting.

Octopuses belong to a division of the Animal Kingdom called Mollusks.
This means they are animals with soft bodies and no bones.
Clams, oysters, and snails are also part of this group.

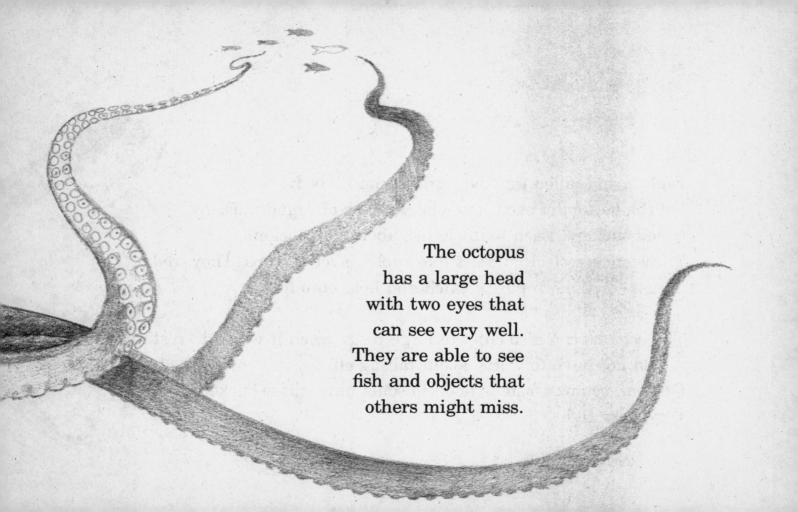

The octopus
has a large head
with two eyes that
can see very well.
They are able to see
fish and objects that
others might miss.

Eight arms called tentacles grow from its body.
On the bottom of each tentacle are rows of round muscles
called suckers. Each tentacle has about 240 suckers.
These suckers look and act like rubber suction cups. They make
it easy for the octopus to catch and hold onto food.

The octopus can also cling to large rocks when it wants to rest
…and not have to worry about falling off.
Once an octopus fastens itself to something, these suckers hold on
very, very tight.

Sometimes the only way to break the grip
is to cut off the tentacle.

But don't worry...
the octopus will
soon grow
a new arm. This special
ability to grow something
new is called *regeneration*.

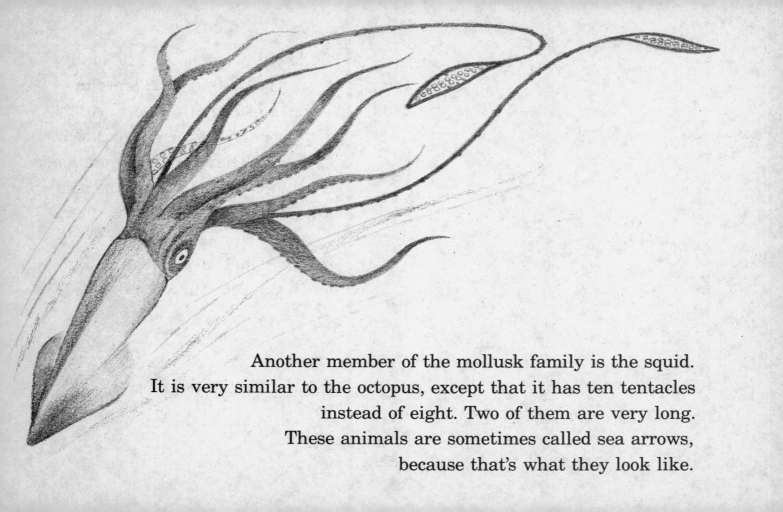

Another member of the mollusk family is the squid.
It is very similar to the octopus, except that it has ten tentacles
instead of eight. Two of them are very long.
These animals are sometimes called sea arrows,
because that's what they look like.

The female octopus lays as many
as 180,000 eggs at one time.
The eggs are attached to rocks
or other hard objects in the sea.
They take two months
to hatch. During this time, the
mother octopus watches over them.
She will not even leave
them long enough to eat. She will go
without food until they are hatched.

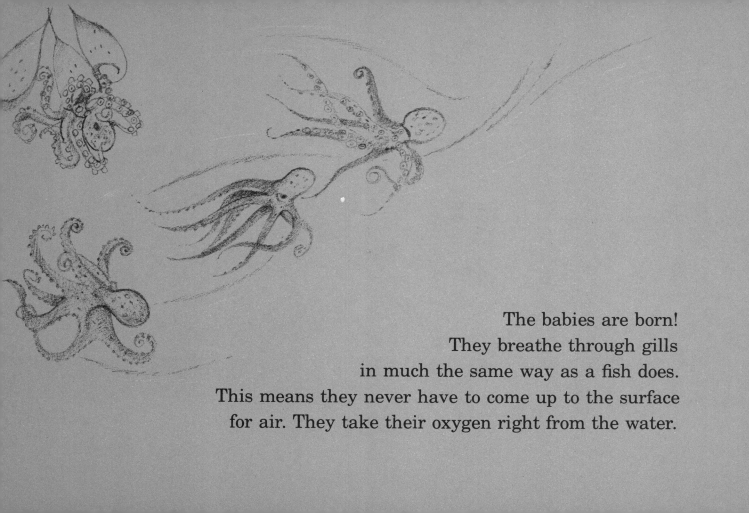

The babies are born!
They breathe through gills
in much the same way as a fish does.
This means they never have to come up to the surface
for air. They take their oxygen right from the water.

The octopus moves through the water
in a slow, wavy motion. The octopus looks like a
graceful ballet dancer as it glides in the ocean.
Each tentacle moves forward and down one at a time.
It moves over and over again until it gets where it's going.

Look Out! Danger!

The octopus has spotted a shark.
The shark is one of its natural enemies.
Now the octopus must use all of its wits and tricks
to escape. When it is scared or in a hurry,
the octopus can move with great speed.

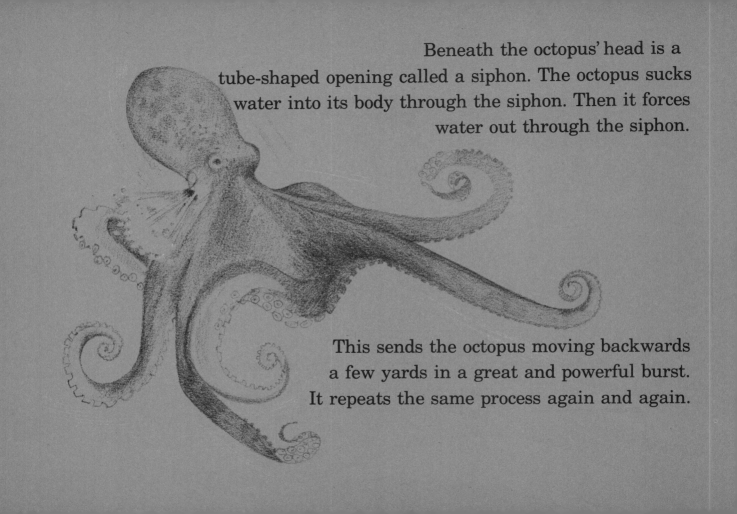

Beneath the octopus' head is a
tube-shaped opening called a siphon. The octopus sucks
water into its body through the siphon. Then it forces
water out through the siphon.

This sends the octopus moving backwards
a few yards in a great and powerful burst.
It repeats the same process again and again.

The shark is getting closer.
It, too, swims with great speed.

Now the octopus uses another of its defenses.
Inside its body is a small sac, filled with a black, inky fluid.
When the octopus squirts the water out
to move quickly, it also squirts
the black, inky fluid.

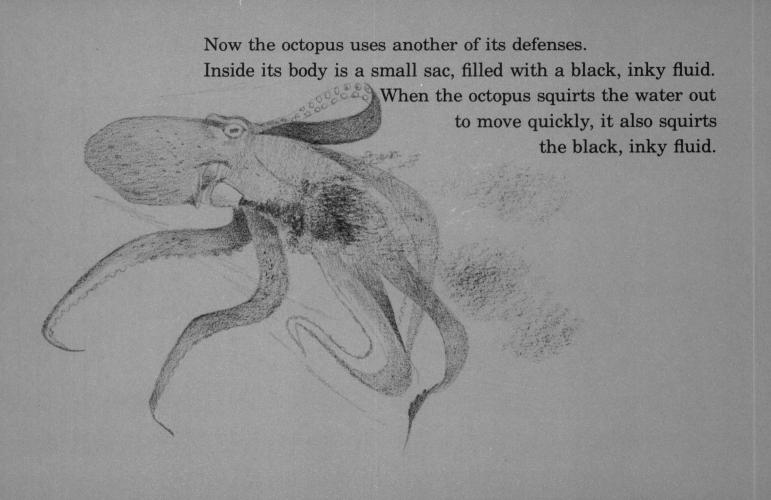

The water turns black and cloudy.
The shark cannot see and becomes confused.
This allows the octopus to swim away without being seen.

The octopus has outwitted the shark.
But just to make sure it is not found again,
the octopus uses still another defense.
Just like a chameleon,
the octopus can change the
coloring of its skin.

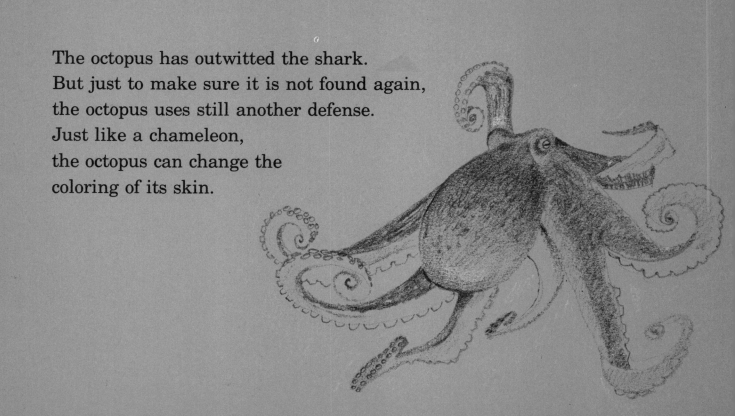

Scientists have found that an octopus' skin contains little bags of
pigment or coloring. When the octopus becomes frightened,
this coloring is released and the skin
is able to change color.

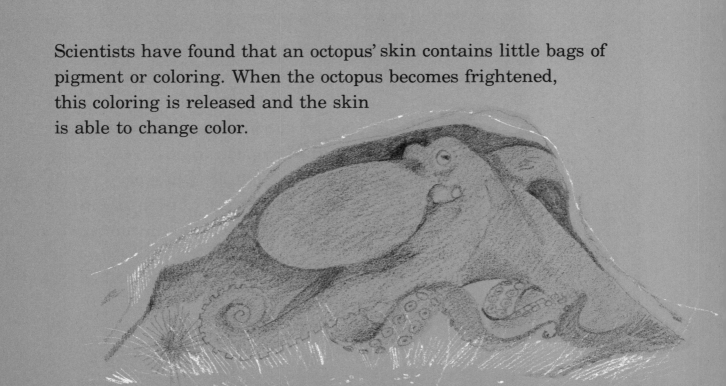

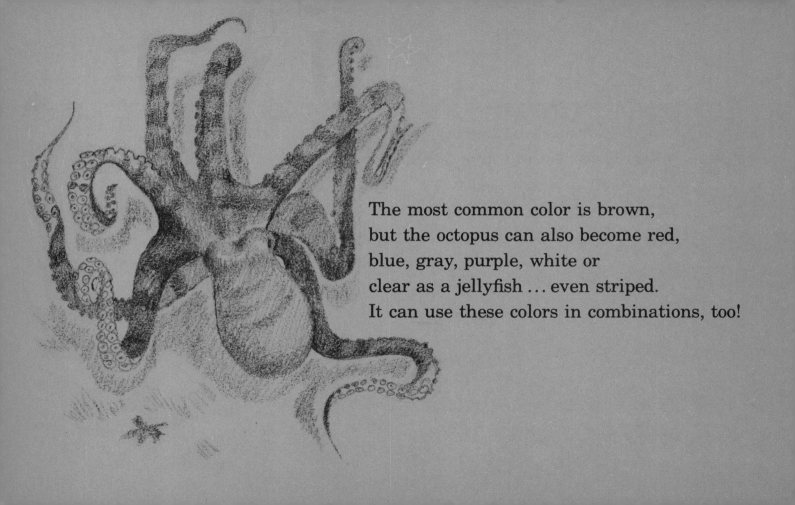

The most common color is brown,
but the octopus can also become red,
blue, gray, purple, white or
clear as a jellyfish ... even striped.
It can use these colors in combinations, too!

Now the octopus decides to hide on the bottom
of the ocean, where it hopes the shark will not see it.
Its skin becomes a sandy brown to match
the bottom of the ocean.

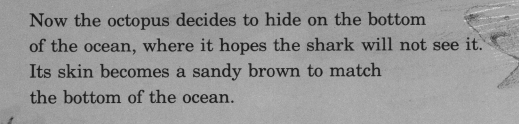

Sure enough, the shark swims right by, looking off
in the distance for the octopus. For the moment,
the danger has passed!

Other natural enemies of the octopus are
big fish, whales and moray eels.

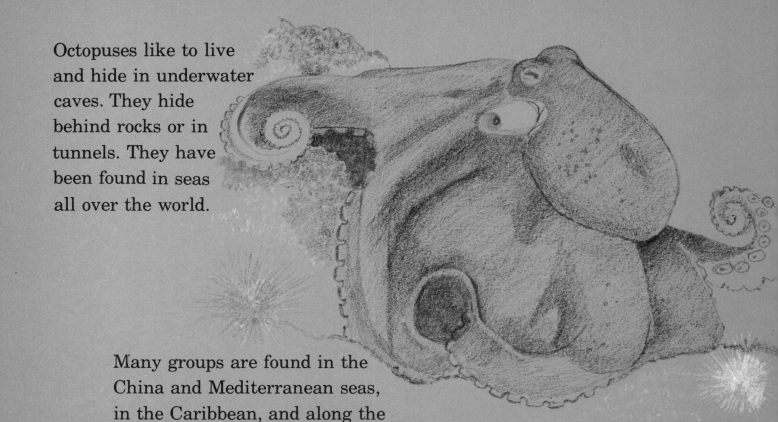

Octopuses like to live
and hide in underwater
caves. They hide
behind rocks or in
tunnels. They have
been found in seas
all over the world.

Many groups are found in the
China and Mediterranean seas,
in the Caribbean, and along the
shores of Hawaii and North America.

Scientists have been able to identify
about 150 kinds of octopuses. They come
in all different sizes. The smallest
is about two inches. Most are the size
of a person's fist.

The Common Octopus lives in the water of the tropics. When it is full grown, it will measure about ten feet across and weigh almost fifty pounds.

The largest of all is the Pacific Octopus.
If you came face to face with this animal,
it would seem like a giant.

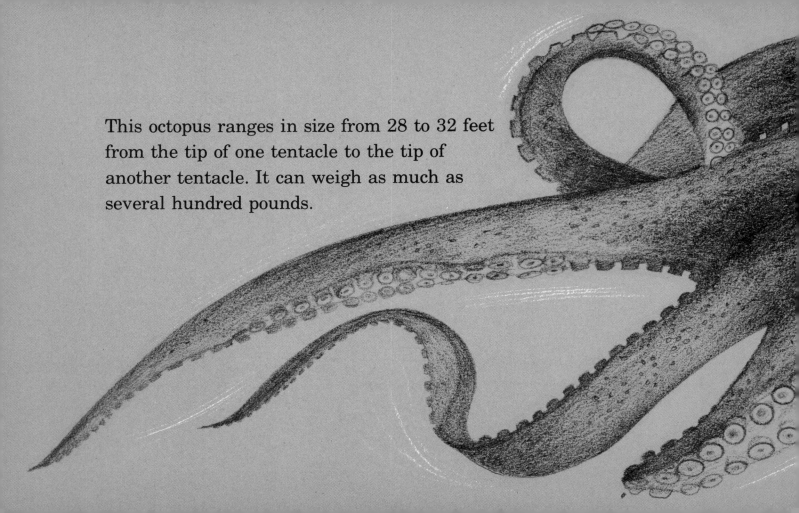

This octopus ranges in size from 28 to 32 feet
from the tip of one tentacle to the tip of
another tentacle. It can weigh as much as
several hundred pounds.

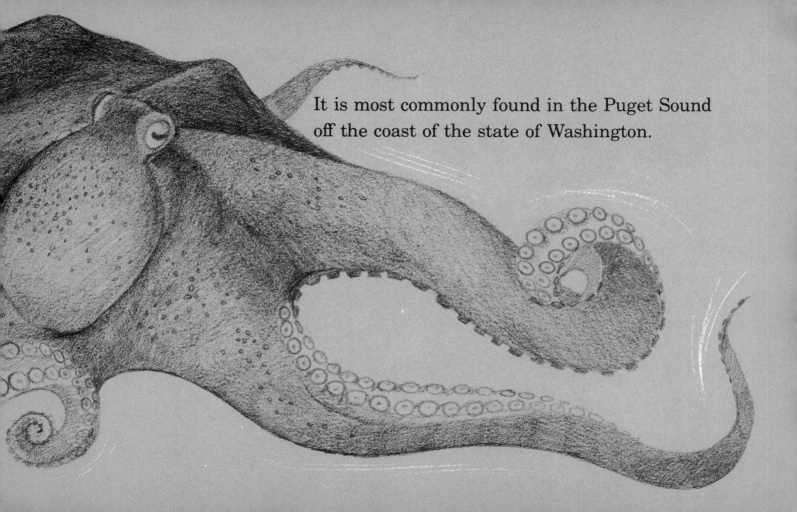

It is most commonly found in the Puget Sound
off the coast of the state of Washington.

When the octopus is hungry,
it likes to feed on other smaller
sea animals, such as the lobster, shrimp,
oyster, and especially the clam and crab.

If the octopus is in a sporting
mood, it will wrap two tentacles
around the shell and pull
it open.

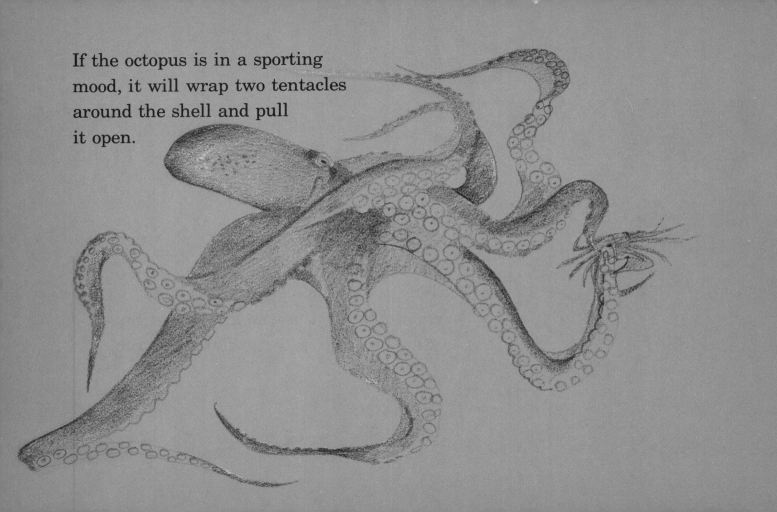

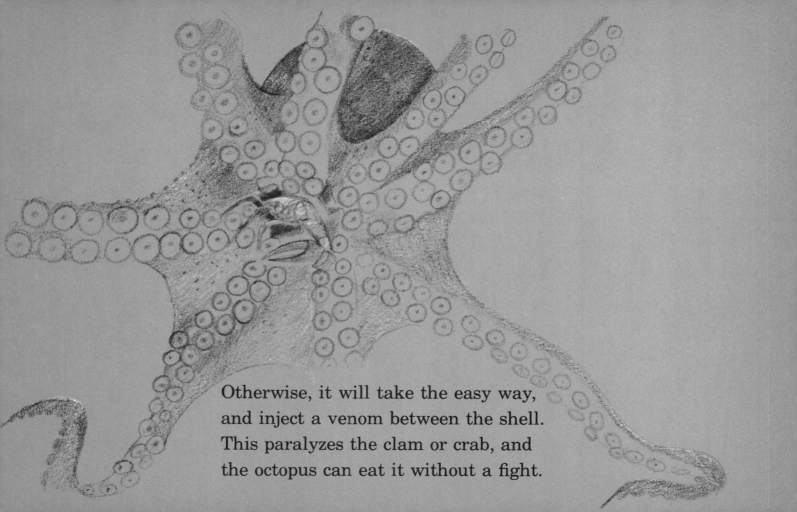

Otherwise, it will take the easy way,
and inject a venom between the shell.
This paralyzes the clam or crab, and
the octopus can eat it without a fight.

The jaw of an octopus
comes to a hard,
sharp, razor-like point,
much like a parrot's beak. This
allows the octopus to easily
grind and chew food.

Almost all octopuses are harmless around people.
But there is a small blue octopus found off the coast of Australia
that has been known to bite. Its venom is poisonous and can kill a
person within several hours. They are only 6 inches, but watch out!

The next time
you go swimming in the ocean
you might have an exciting experience.
You might see an octopus. But you won't be
frightened because now you know all about them.

You'll probably agree
that they are one of the most
interesting creatures
of the deep, dark sea.